First Facts®

PREDATOR PROFILES

GRIZZLY BEARS

— BUILT FOR THE HUNT —

by Lori Polydoros

Consultant: Dr. Jackie Gai, DVM
Wildlife Veterinarian

CAPSTONE PRESS
a capstone imprint

First Facts are published by Capstone Press,
1710 Roe Crest Drive, North Mankato, Minnesota 56003
www.capstonepub.com

Library of Congress Cataloging-in-Publication Data
Cataloging-in-Publication Data is on file with the Library of Congress.
ISBN 978-1-4914-5043-7 (library binding)
ISBN 978-1-4914-5085-7 (eBook PDF)

Editorial Credits
Brenda Haugen, editor; Juliette Peters, designer; Tracy Cummins,
media researcher; Katy LaVigne, production specialist

Photo Credits
Getty Images: Barrett Hedges, 19, Don Johnston, 17; Minden Pictures: Michio Hoshino, 1,
15; Shutterstock: AndreAnita, 11, Galyna Andrushko, 12, Gleb Tarro, 8, 13, Greg and Jan
Ritchie, 14, Jeffrey B. Banke, 3, Jim David, 2, 10, Nagel Photography, Cover, pashabo, Design
Element, riekephotos, 6, saraporn, 7, Scott E Read, Cover Back, 5, 9; SuperStock: Animals
Animals, 21.

Printed in China by Nordica
0415/CA21500544
042015   008845NORDF15

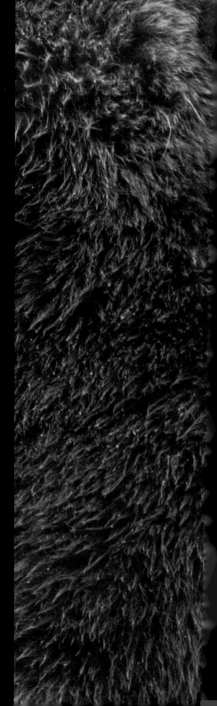

TABLE OF CONTENTS

On the Menu 4

Expert Sniffers 6

Look and Listen 8

Dangerously Fast 10

A Fishy Feast 12

Dig It 14

Grind It Up 16

Surprise Attack! 18

What's that Smell? 20

Amazing but True! 20

Glossary 22

Read More 23

Internet Sites 23

Critical Thinking Using
   the Common Core 24

Index 24

ON THE MENU

Grizzly bears are built to live and hunt in harsh, cold places. The bears have powerful bodies and thick fur. They live in parts of Canada and the northwestern United States.

Grizzly bears are **omnivores**. They hunt **prey**, such as deer, moose, and fish. They also eat berries, insects, and dead animals.

FACT

Only about 1,000 grizzlies remain in the United States, outside of Alaska. People use more land where the bears once lived. Because of that, fewer grizzlies are born each year.

omnivore—an animal that eats plants and other animals

prey—an animal hunted by another animal for food

EXPERT SNIFFERS

Grizzly bears are deadly **predators** with a sharp sense of smell. They bow their heads low and sniff as they walk. Grizzlies sniff for prey and other food. They can smell an animal **carcass** from about 2 miles (3 kilometers) away.

FACT

A grizzly's sense of smell is seven times better than that of a bloodhound. Police sometimes use bloodhounds to track the **scents** of criminals or missing people.

predator—an animal that hunts other animals for food

carcass—the body of a dead animal

scent—the smell of something

LOOK AND LISTEN

Grizzlies have good vision. They see about as well as people do. But grizzly bears see even better at night. They often stand on their back legs to look for prey.

Grizzlies hear twice as well as people do. They also can hear in all directions. A young grizzly bear's round ears grow to full size before the rest of its body. Grizzlies can hear prey in a thick forest.

FACT
A grizzly's ear has a balloon-shaped bone that makes sounds louder.

DANGEROUSLY FAST

With strong upper bodies, grizzlies can power across land. A big shoulder hump made of muscle makes a grizzly fast and strong. A grizzly can chase prey at speeds of 35 miles (56 km) per hour. With their strength, grizzlies can easily overpower their prey.

FACT

Grizzlies can be 10 feet (3 meters) tall when standing on their back legs. They can weigh up to 1,200 pounds (544 kilograms).

A FISHY FEAST

Fish is a main menu item for grizzlies living in the northwestern United States. Grizzlies are powerful swimmers. They swim in rivers full of salmon. The salmon swim upstream to lay eggs. Grizzlies catch the fish right in their mouths! The bears can eat more than 100 pounds (45 kg) of salmon each day.

DIG IT

Grizzly bears have sharp claws that grow about 4 inches (10 centimeters) long. The bears use their claws to grip prey. They also dig up plants and rip open logs. These diggers can destroy **burrows** to reach squirrels or mice. Their powerful legs and paws can break bones in one swipe.

FACT

Grizzlies also use their paws to move rocks. They uncover moths hiding there. A grizzly can eat 20,000 moths a day!

burrow—a tunnel or hole in the ground made or used by an animal

GRIND IT UP

A grizzly bear can bite hard enough to crush a bowling ball or bite through an iron frying pan. It uses its 42 strong, sharp teeth to tear and grind food. A grizzly bear has a huge mouth that can open up almost as wide as a ruler.

FACT

Grizzlies have deadly **canine** teeth. These teeth work like scissors to shred meat.

canine—a long, pointed tooth

SURPRISE ATTACK!

A grizzly bear sometimes **ambushes** its prey. It might **stalk** a group of North American elk. The bear will attack with a burst of speed. The grizzly will aim for a young elk trailing behind the herd. The bear uses its fierce paws to knock down the animal. The grizzly bear kills its prey quickly.

ambush—to attack by surprise
stalk—to hunt an animal in a secret, quiet way

WHAT'S THAT SMELL?

Grizzlies stink but for a good reason. The bears rub their bodies over dead animals to hide their own smell. Then they can sneak around without their prey knowing they are near. This makes the bears even more dangerous to their prey!

AMAZING BUT TRUE!

Grizzly bears **hibernate** for up to seven months each year. To get ready to hibernate, the bears eat extra food and double their body fat. They do not eat, drink, or go to the bathroom during hibernation. Their heartbeats slow from 40 beats a minute to just 8 beats a minute.

hibernate—to spend winter in a deep sleep

A grizzly bear hibernates in a den.

GLOSSARY

ambush (AM-bush)—attack by surprise

burrow (BUHR-oh)—a tunnel or hole in the ground made or used by an animal

canine (KAY-nyn)—a long, pointed tooth

carcass (KAHR-kuhs)—the body of a dead animal

hibernate (HYE-bur-nate)—to spend winter in a deep sleep

omnivore (OM-nuh-vor)—an animal that eats plants and other animals

predator (PRED-uh-tur)—an animal that hunts other animals for food

prey (PRAY)—an animal hunted by another animal for food

scent (SENT)—the smell of something

stalk (STAWK)—to hunt an animal in a secret, quiet way

READ MORE

Arnosky, Jim. *Tooth and Claw: The Wild World of Big Predators.* New York: Sterling Children's Books, 2014.

Kolpin, Molly. *Grizzly Bears.* Bears. Mankato, Minn.: Capstone Press, 2012.

Maday, Gregory. *Hunting with Grizzly Bears.* Animal Attack! New York: Gareth Stevens Publishing, 2013.

Miller, Debbie S. *Grizzly Bears of Alaska.* Seattle: Sasquatch Books, 2014.

INTERNET SITES

FactHound offers a safe, fun way to find Internet sites related to this book. All of the sites on FactHound have been researched by our staff.

Here's all you do:

Visit *www.facthound.com*

Type in this code: 9781491450437

 Check out projects, games and lots more at **www.capstonekids.com**

CRITICAL THINKING
USING THE COMMON CORE

1. How do grizzly bears use their senses to hunt? (Key Ideas and Details)

2. What makes grizzly bears well suited for living and hunting in cold weather? (Integration of Knowledge and Ideas)

INDEX

Alaska, 4

bloodhounds, 6
burrows, 14

Canada, 4
carcasses, 6

forests, 8

grizzly bears
  claws, 14
  diet, 4, 12, 14, 20
  ears, 8
  fur, 4
  heartbeats, 20
  hibernating, 20
  hiding their smell, 20

legs, 8, 10, 14
mouths, 16
paws, 14, 18
senses, 6, 8
shoulder humps, 10
size, 10
speed, 10, 18
stalking, 18
swimming, 12
teeth, 16

omnivores, 4

rivers, 12

United States, 4, 12